Philosophy of Recreation

Philosophy of Recreation

George J. Romanes
Benjamin W. Richardson

LM Publishers

The Science and Philosophy of Recreation[1]

In all places of the civilized world, and in all classes of the civilized community, the struggle for existence is now more keen than ever it has been during the history of our race. Everywhere men, and women, and children are living at a pressure positively frightful to contemplate. Amid the swarming bustle of our smoke-smothered towns, surrounded by their zone of poisoned trees, amid the whirling roar of machinery, the scorching blast of furnaces, and in the tallow-lighted blackness of our mines— everywhere, over all the length and breadth of this teeming land, men, and women, and children, in no metaphor, but in cruel truth, are struggling for life. Even our smiling landscapes support as the sons of their soil a new generation, to whom the freedom of gladness is

---

[1] By George J. Romanes (1848–1894).

a tradition of the past, and on whose brows is stamped, not only the print of honest work, but a new and sadding mark—the brand of sickening care. Or if we look to our universities and schools, to our professional men and men of business, we see this same fierce battle rage—ruined health and shattered hopes, tearful lives and early deaths being everywhere the bitter lot of millions who toil, and strive, and love, and bleed their young hearts' blood in sorrow. In such a world and at such a time, when more truly than ever it may be said that the whole creation groans in pain and travail, I do not know that for the purposes of health and happiness there is any subject which it is more desirable that persons of all classes should understand than the philosophical theory and the rational practice of recreation. For recreation is the great relief from the pressure of life—the breathing-space in the daily struggle for existence, without which no one of the combatants could long survive; and therefore it becomes of the first importance that the science and the philosophy of such relief should be generally known. No doubt it is true that people will always be compelled to take recreation and to profit by its use, whether or not they are acquainted with its science and its philosophy; but there can be equally little doubt that here, as elsewhere, an intelligent understanding of abstract principles as well as of practical applications will insure more use and less abuse of the thing which is thus intelligently understood.

With a view, then, of obtaining some such intelligent understanding of recreation, let us begin by clearly understanding what recreation means. First of all, the mere word, like many of our other English words that signify abstractions, condenses much philosophy within itself. For, as "creation" means a forming, "re-creation" means a forming anew; and, as in etymological derivation, so in actual truth re-creation is nothing other than a re-novation of the vital energies; leisure time and appropriate employment serve to repair the organic machinery which has been impaired by the excess of work. The literal meaning of the word is therefore in itself instructive, as showing that what our forefathers saw in recreation was not so much play, pastime, or pleasantry, as the restoration of enfeebled powers of work. And I do not know that within the limits of one word they could have left us a legacy of thought more true in itself or more solemn in its admonition. Recreation is, *or ought to be,* not a pastime entered upon for the sake of the pleasure which it affords, but an act of duty undertaken for the sake of the subsequent power which it generates, and the subsequent profit which it insures. Therefore, expanding the philosophy which is thus condensed in our English word, we may define recreation as that which with the least expenditure of time renders the exhausted energies most fitted to resume their work. Such is my definition of recreation; yet I know that many things are called by this name which can not possibly fall within this definition, and I doubt whether nine persons out of ten ever dreamed either of attaching such a meaning to the word, or of applying such a principle to the thing. Nevertheless, I also know that in whatever degree so-called recreation fails to be covered by this definition, in that degree does it fail, properly speaking, to be recreation at all. It may be amusement, fun, or even profitable employment; but it is not that particular thing which it is the object of this paper to consider. Therefore the definition which I have laid down may be taken as a practical test of recreation as genuine or spurious. If recreation is of a kind that renders a man less fitted for work than would some other kind of occupation, or if it consumes more time than would some other kind of occupation which would secure an equal amount of recuperation, then, in whatever degree this is so, in that degree must the quality of such recreation be pronounced impure.

So much, then, for the meaning of recreation. The next point that I shall consider is the physiology of recreation. It may have struck some readers as a curious question, why some actions or pursuits should present what I may call a recreative character, and others not. For it is evident that this character is by no means determined by the relief from *labor* which these actions or pursuits secure. A week on the moors involves more genuine hard work than does a week in the mines, and a game of chess may require as much effort of thought as a problem in high mathematics. Moreover, the same action or pursuit may vary in its recreative quality with different individuals. Rowing, which is the favorite recreation of the undergraduate, is serious work to the bargeman; and we never find a gardener to resemble his master in showing a partiality to digging for digging's sake. If it is suggested that it is the need of bodily exercise which renders muscular activity beneficial to the one class and not to the other, I answer, no doubt it is so partly, but not wholly;

for why is it that a man of science should find recreation in reading history, while an historian finds recreation in the pursuit of science? or why is it that a London tradesman should find a beneficial holiday in the country, while a country tradesman finds a no less beneficial holiday in London? The truth seems to me to be that the only principle which will serve to explain the recreative quality in all cases is what I may call the physiological necessity for frequent change of organic activity, and the consequent physiological value of variety in the kinds and seasons of such activity. In order to render this principle perfectly clear, it will be necessary for me very briefly to explain the physiology of nutrition.

When food is taken into the body it undergoes a variety of processes which are collectively called digestion and assimilation. Into the details of these processes I need not enter, it being enough for my present purpose to say that the total result of these processes is to strain off the nutritious constituents of the food, and pour them into the current of the blood. The blood circulates through nearly all the tissues of the body, being contained in a closed system of tubes. This system of tubes springs from the heart in the form of large, hollow trunks which ramify into smaller and smaller tube-branches. These are all called arteries. The smaller arteries again ramify into a countless meshwork of so-called capillaries. Capillaries are also closed tubes, but differ from arteries in being immensely more numerous, more slender, and more tenuous in their walls. These capillaries pervade the body in such an intimate meshwork that a needle's point cannot be run into any part of the body where they occur without destroying the integrity of some of them, and so causing an outflow of blood.

As these capillaries ramify from the arteries, so do they again coalesce into larger tubes, and these into larger, and so on, until all this system of return tubing ends again in the heart in the form of large, hollow trunks. The tubes composing this system of return tubing are called the veins. Thus the whole blood-vascular system may be likened to two trees which are throughout joined together by their leaves, and also by cavities at the bottoms of their trunks—the heart. The branches of both trees being everywhere hollow, the contained fluid runs up the stem, and through smaller and smaller branches of the arterial tree, into the delicate vessels of the leaves, which may be taken to represent the capillaries. Passing through these into the twigs of the venous tree, the blood returns through larger and larger branches of this tree till it arrives at the trunk, and completes its circuit by again entering the trunk of the arterial tree through the cavities of the heart. Now the blood, in perpetually making this complete circuit of the body, performs three important functions: it serves to carry oxygen from the lungs to all the other parts of the body; it serves to supply all parts of the body with the nutritive material with which it is charged; and it serves to drain off from all the tissues of the body the effete products which they excrete, and to present these effete products to the organs whose function it is again to abstract them from the blood and expel them from the body. The two latter functions of the blood—those of nourishing and draining—I must consider more in detail. They are both performed in the capillaries, so that the object of the arteries and veins may be considered as merely that of conveying the blood to and from the capillaries. Moreover, both functions are performed by transfusion through the delicate walls of the capillaries—the nutritive material in the blood being thus transfused into the surrounding tissues, and the waste product of these tissues being transfused into the blood. Thus, in the various vascular tissues there is always a double process going on: first, that of receiving nourishment from the blood, whereby they are being constantly built up into an efficient state for the performance of their various functions; and, secondly, that of discharging into the blood the effete materials which the performance of these functions entails. Now, when any tissue or organ is in a state of activity in the performance of its function, the activity which it manifests entails a process of disintegration, which is the reverse of the process of nutrition; that is to say, when a tissue or organ is doing its work, it is expending energy which it has previously derived in virtue of the process of nutrition. Work is therefore, so to speak, the using up of nutrition; so that if the income of energy due to nutrition is equal to the expenditure of energy due to work, the tissue or organ will remain stationary as regards its capacity for further work, while, if the work done is in excess of the nutrition supplied, the tissue or organ will soon be unable to continue its work; it will become, as we say, exhausted, cease to work, and remain passive until it is again slowly and gradually refreshed or built up by the process of nutrition. Therefore all the tissues and organs of the body require periods of rest to alternate with periods of activity; and what is true of each part of the body is likewise true of the body as a whole—sleep being nothing other than a time of general rest during which the process of nutrition is allowed to gain upon that of exhaustion. Thus we may have local exhaustion—as when the muscles of our arm are no longer able to hold out a heavy weight—or we may have general exhaustion, as in sleep; and we may have local restorations due to nutrition—as when our exhausted arm, after some interval of rest, is again able to sustain the weight—or we may have a general restoration due to nutrition, as in the effects of sleep.

I have now said enough about the physiology of nutrition to render quite clear what I mean by recreation depending on the physiological necessity for a frequent change of organic activity. For although in the case of some organs—such as most of the secreting organs— activity is pretty constant, owing to the constant expenditure of energy being just about balanced by the constant income, in the case of nerves and muscles this is not so; during the times when these organs are in activity their expenditure of energy is so vastly greater than their income during the same times, that they can only do their work by drawing upon the stores of energy which have been laid up by them during the comparatively long periods of their previous rest. Now, recreation applies only to nerve and muscle; and what it amounts to is simply this—a change of organic activity, having for its object the affording of time for the nutrition of exhausted portions of the body. A part of the body having become exhausted by work done, and yet the whole of the body not being exhausted so far as to require sleep, recreation is the affording of local sleep to the exhausted part by transferring the scene of activity from it to some other part. Be it observed that a certain amount of activity is necessary for the life and health of all the organs of the body; so it would not do for the community of organs as a whole that, when any one set become exhausted by their own activity, all the others should share in their time of rest, as in general sleep. But, by transferring the state of activity from organs already exhausted by work to organs which are ready nourished to perform work, recreation may be termed, as I have said, local sleep.

Thus we see that, in a physiological no less than in a psychological sense, the term re-creation is a singularly happy one; for we see that, as a matter of fact, the whole physiology of recreation consists merely of a re-building up, re-forming, or re-creation of tissues which have become partly broken down by the exhausting effects of work. So that in this physiological sense recreation is partial sleep, while sleep is universal recreation. And now we see why it is that the one essential principle of all recreation must be that of variety of organic activity; for variety of organic activity merely means the substitution of one set of organic activities for another, and consequently the successive affording of rest to bodily structures as they are successively exhausted. The undergraduate finds recreation in rowing because it gives his brain time to recover its exhausted energies, while the historian and the man of science find recreation in each other's labors because these labors require somewhat different faculties of mind for their pursuance.

Before concluding these general remarks on the physiology of recreation, I must say a few words with more special reference to the physiology of exercise. We do not require science to teach us that the most lucrative form of recreation for those whose labor is not of a bodily kind is muscular exercise. Why this should be so is sufficiently obvious. The movement of blood in the veins is due to two causes.

The act of drawing breath into the lungs, by dilating the closed cavity of the chest, serves also to draw venous blood into the heart. This cause of the onward movement of blood in the veins is what is called aspiration, and it occurs also in some of the larger veins of the limbs, which are so situated with reference to their supplying branches that movement of the limbs determines suction of the blood from the supplying branches to the veins. The second great cause of the venous flow is as follows: The larger veins are nearly all provided with valves which open to allow the blood to pass on toward the heart, but close against the blood if it endeavors to return back toward the capillaries. Now, the larger veins are imbedded in muscles, so that the effect of muscular contractions is to compress numberless veins now in one part and now in another part of their length; and, as each vein is thus compressed, its contained fluid is, of course, driven forward from valve to valve. Hence, as all the veins of the body end in the heart, the total effect of general muscular activity is greatly to increase the flow of venous blood into the heart. The heart is thus stimulated to greater activity in order to avoid being gorged with the unusual inflow of blood. So great is the increase of the heart's activity that is required to meet this sudden demand on its powers of propulsion, that everyone can feel in his own person how greatly muscular exercise increases the number of the heart's contractions. Now, the result of this increase of the heart's activity is, of course, to pump a correspondingly greater amount of blood into the arteries, and so to quicken the circulation all over the body. This, in turn, gives rise to a greater amount of tissue-change—oxygenation, nutrition, and drainage—which, together with the increased discharge of carbonic acid by the muscles during their time of increased activity, has the effect of unduly charging the blood with carbonic acid and other effete materials. This increased amount of carbonic acid in the blood stimulates the respiratory center in the spinal cord to increase the frequency of the respiratory movements, so that under the influence of violent and sustained exercise we become, as it is expressively said, "out of breath." The distress to which this condition may give rise is, however, chiefly due to the heart being unable to deliver blood into the arteries as quickly as it receives blood from the veins; the result being a more or less undue pressure of venous blood upon a heart already struggling to its utmost to pump on all the blood it can. Training, which is chiefly systematic exercise, by promoting a healthy concordant action between the heart and arteries, diminishes the resistance which the latter offer to an unusual flow of blood from the former, and therefore men in training, or men accustomed to bodily exercise, do not easily become distressed by sustained muscular exertion.

Now it is evident, without comment, how immense must be the benefit of muscular exercise. Not only does it allow time for the brain to rest when exhausted by mental work, but, by increasing the circulation all over the body, it promotes the threefold function of oxygenation, nutrition, and drainage. It thus refreshes the whole organism in all its parts; it increases by use the strength and endurance of the muscles; it maintains the heart and the lungs—or rather the whole of the circulatory and respiratory mechanisms—at the highest point of their natural efficiency; and, in general, next only to air and food, muscular exercise is of all things most essential to the vitality of the organism.

So much, then, for the physiology of recreation; and, having said this much on the abstract principles of our subject, I shall devote the rest of my paper to a consideration of this subject in its more practical aspects.

The fundamental principle of all recreation consisting, as I have said, in the rest from local exhaustion which is secured by a change of organic activity, it is clear that practical advice with regard to recreation must differ widely according to the class, and even the individual, to which it is given. Thus it would be clearly absurd to recommend a literary man, already jaded with mental work, to adopt as his means of recreation some sedentary form of amusement; while it would be no less absurd to recommend a workingman, already fatigued with bodily toil, to regale himself with athletics. And, in lower degrees, the kind and amount of recreation which it would be wise to recommend must differ with different individuals in the same class of society, according to their age, sex, temperament, pursuits, and previous habits of life. But, although all matters of detail thus require to be adjusted to individual cases, there is one practical consideration which applies equally to all cases, and which must never be lost sight of if recreation of any kind is to produce its full measure of result. This consideration is the all-important part which is played in recreation by the emotions. It is, I am sure, impossible to over-estimate the value of the emotions in this connection—a prolonged flow of happy feelings doing more to brace up the system for work than any other influence operating for a similar length of time. The physiological reasons why this should be so are not apparent; for, although we know that the emotions have a very powerful influence in stimulating the nerves which act on the various secreting organs of the body, I do not think that this fact alone is sufficient to explain the high value of pleasurable emotions in refreshing the nervous system. There must be some further reason— probably to be sought for within the limits of the nervous system itself—why a flow of happy feelings serves to re-create the nervous energies. But, be the reasons what they may, we must never neglect to remember the fact that the influence of all others most detrimental to recreation is the absence of agreeable emotions or the presence of painful ones. There is, for instance, comparatively little use in taking so-called constitutional exercise at stated times, if the mind during these times is emotionally colorless, or, still worse, aching with sorrow and care. If recreation is to be of good quality, it must before all things be of a kind to stimulate pleasurable feelings, and while it lasts it ought to engross the whole of our consciousness. Half-hearted action is quite as little remunerative here as elsewhere; and, if we desire to work well, no less in play than in work must we fulfill the saying, "What thy hand findeth to do, do it with thy might."

Having stated this practical principle as of paramount importance in all recreation, I shall devote the rest of my space to giving a variety of suggestions concerning the recreation of all classes of society; and, for the sake of securing method to my discussion, I shall primarily consider the community in its most natural classes of men, women, and children.

There is not much to be said on the recreation of men belonging to the upper classes. That most objectionable of creatures, the gentleman at large without occupation, has a free choice before him of every amusement that the world has to give; but one thing he is hopelessly denied—the keen enjoyment of recreation. Living from year to year in a round of varied pastimes, he becomes slowly incapacitated for forming habits of work, while at the same time he is slowly sapping all the enjoyment from play. For, although variety of amusement may please for a time, it is notorious that it cannot do so indefinitely. The intellectual changes which are involved in changes of amusement are not sufficiently pronounced to re-create even the faculties on which the sense of amusement depends; the mind, therefore, becomes surfeited with amusement of all kinds, just as it may become surfeited with a tune too constantly played— even though the tune be played in frequently changing keys. For such men, if past middle life, I have no advice to give. They have placed themselves beyond the possibility of finding recreation, and their only use in the world is to show the doom of idleness. They, more even than paupers, are the parasites of the social organism; and we can scarcely regret that their lumpish life, being one of stagnation self-induced, should be one of miserable failure, to the wretchedness of which we can extend no hope.

Turning next to gentlemen of active pursuits, I may most fitly begin with those who are beginning life at the universities. At our larger universities both the provisions for recreation and the manner in which they are used are in a high degree satisfactory, and ought to serve as a model to universities all over the world. It may be true that at the Continental universities rowing would not inspire a tenth part of the enthusiasm which it creates at Oxford and Cambridge; and I know from experience that it is hopeless to persuade German students, as a class, to adopt what they consider childish toys—the bats and balls of cricket. All I can say is, so much the worse for the Continental universities. In everything that appertains to work—and more especially to original work—I am profoundly convinced that the sooner we copy something from the German universities the better; but, in most things that appertain to play, the English universities constitute the best models. Rowing, cricket, football, athletics, and, in a lower degree, gymnastics, bicycling, swimming, and riding, constitute, besides walking, the favorite modes of exercise; and it is impossible to suggest better. I have only to object that, regarded as recreation, there is, both at Oxford and Cambridge, far too much tendency to a specialization of these forms of exercise. Competition dictates practice, and practice entails too exclusive a devotion to the one kind of exercise which is practiced; so that, as a consequence, there is too sharp a division between the boating-men, the cricketers, and the athletes for securing the full benefit of exercise which all would derive if they were more usually to participate in one another's pursuits. But this evil is to some extent unavoidable, as it arises immediately from the spirit of emulation, without which the mere exercise would lose its zest, and so the fullness of its recreative value. Still, now that so many of the colleges are provided with their own cricket-grounds, and the boats are practically open to all, there is no reason why even the most ambitious aspirants to the "'varsity blue" should not enjoy more variety of exercise than is usually the case.

In the army and navy there is abundant time for recreation, which is too frequently wasted in mere lounging. When once the army or navy examinations are passed, there is comparatively little mental work required in the performance of duty, and therefore the comparatively large amount of leisure time which officers enjoy ought to be much more generally devoted than it is to reading, or even to original work. Officers constitute a class presenting no small proportion of intelligent members; so that the comparative rareness with which they present either high culture or proved powers of original work must, I think, be set down to a general bad habit or fashion of substituting idle amusement for profitable recreation.

To professional men, men of business, and indeed all who are engaged in pursuits requiring more or less severe mental work, coupled with more or less confinement, exercise is, of course, the *conditio sine qua non* of the recreation to be recommended. This fact is so obvious that I need not dwell upon it further than to make one remark. This is to warn all such persons that their feelings are no safe guide as to the amount of muscular exercise that is requisite for maintaining full and *sustained* health. By habitual neglect of sufficient exercise the system may and does accommodate itself to such neglect; so that not only may the desire for exercise cease to be a fair measure of its need, but positive exhaustion may attend a much less amount of exercise than is necessary to long continuance of sound health. However strong and well, therefore, a man may feel notwithstanding his neglect of exercise, he ought to remember that he is playing a most dangerous game, and that sooner or later his sin will find him out—either in the form of dyspepsia, liver, kidney, or other disease, which so surely creep upon the offender against Nature's laws of health. According to Dr. Parkes, the amount of exercise that a healthy man ought to take without fatigue is at the least that which is required for raising 150 foot-tons per diem. This, in mere walking, would, in the case of a man of ordinary weight, be represented by a walk of between eight and nine miles along level ground, or one mile up a tolerably steep hill; but it is desirable that the requisite amount of exercise should be obtained without throwing all the work upon one set of muscles. For this reason walking ought to be varied with rowing, riding, active games, and, where practicable, hunting or shooting, which, to those who are fond of sport, constitute the most perfect form of recreative exercise.

Turning next to all the large class of men below the grade of clerks, their possible means of recreation are alike in this—that they must be more or less of a corporate kind. These men depend for their recreation on public institutions, and therefore it is of the first importance to the national health, happiness, morals, and intelligence that no thought, pains, or money should be spared in providing such institutions, adequate in number and competent in character to meet so important and so immense a need. Within the limits of so general an essay it is impossible to do anything like justice to this subject; but I may say a few words on the kinds of institutions that I should most like to recommend.

Every town the size of which is so considerable that green grass and fresh air are not within easy reach of all its inhabitants, ought at any expense to be provided with public parks. In many of our large towns it is now virtually impracticable to provide such parks in central situations; but even suburban parks are infinitely better than no parks at all. Public recreation-grounds having been provided, every inducement ought to be added to attract the people to use them. Gymnasia, boating, cricket and golf implements, lawn-tennis, and tennis-courts, ought all to be supplied at the public expense, so that workingmen and boys might be able to spend their holidays and half-holidays in healthy outdoor amusement without requiring to incur the expense of club subscriptions. Outdoor clubs, however, ought not the less to be encouraged for the sake of the additional inducement which *esprit de corps* and competition give to outdoor recreation—the club subscriptions being limited to the providing of prizes. Bands ought also to be provided at the public expense to play in the parks during the spring and summer months on the afternoons of holidays and Sundays. The importance of this latter provision cannot be too highly rated; for experience shows that wherever it has been tried its success has been astonishing. For instance, Lord Thurlow, quoting from Sir Benjamin Hall, stated to the House of Lords, on the 5th of May, that the

Sunday visitors to Kensington Gardens had, by the band playing there, been increased from 7,000 to 80,000 in one day, and in the Regent's and Victoria Parks 190,000 had been attracted by the bands in one afternoon. When we consider what an amount of health, happiness, and refining influence these numbers represent as produced by a single cause, we blush for the narrow fanaticism which, in the name of religion, does all it can to deny to the working-classes the elevating influence of music on the only day that the toil of life admits of their obtaining it. I hold it to be impossible too strongly to deprecate the downright immorality of driving the working-classes by thousands into the pot-houses by depriving them of the innocent and refining enjoyment of music in the open air. Surely the common sense of the public, as a whole, is not so degraded by bigotry that, in the face of the figures I have quoted, there can any longer be a question in the public mind on the positive sin of allowing a puritanical spirit in the few to domineer over the health, the happiness, and the morals of the many.

Somewhat similar remarks apply to the question of opening museums and art-galleries on Sundays, though on this question the Sabbatarians include among their ranks a greater proportional number of the community. In the debate of 'the 5th of May, to which I have already alluded, both Church and State, in so far as they are represented in the persons of the Primate and the Premier, spoke strongly against any reform in this direction; and, perhaps owing to this weight of united authority, the proposed reform was negatived by a majority of eight. Yet, when we examine the arguments which these high authorities were able to produce, we find them to be conspicuously of the feeblest kind. The leading argument both of the Prime Minister and of the Archbishop was that there is not sufficient evidence "of a very predominant sentiment" in favor of the reform on the part of workingmen themselves. Now, to this it may be answered; in the first place, that a poll on the question has not been taken, and that, therefore, it is a mere begging of the question to say that workingmen as a class "in all probability" do not desire the change. But, even if we grant that the working-classes as a whole are as apathetic upon the subject as they are represented to be, I do not see that this is any valid reason against reform. Possibly enough, the members of the House of Lords have a higher appreciation of the value of science-museums and art-galleries, as well as the privileges and advantages of entering them, than have the members of workingmen's clubs; and I doubt not that, if the upper and the lower classes were for a few months to change places, petitions to Parliament of the kind which Lord Thurlow presented would be more numerous and more generally signed. But what does this argue? Surely not that we, who best know the culturing value of these institutions, ought to use the comparative ignorance of those who do not as an argument against extending to them the opportunity of ascertaining that value. On the contrary, in whatever degree indifference can be proved of the working-classes in this matter, it would seem to me a strong argument in favor of instilling into them a more lively perception of the educational advantages of such institutions; and this can only be done by throwing open these institutions on the (virtually) one day in the week when the classes in question are able to visit them. Of course, it may be said that the alleged indifference arises, not from ignorance of the value of such institutions, but from a preponderant sense of Sabbatarianism on the part of the working-classes. But, supposing the alleged apathy to exist, and supposing it to arise from the latter cause alone—which I deem highly improbable—I still think it would constitute no valid argument against the proposed reform. We are all, I take it, agreed upon the recreative as well as what Lord Beaconsfield called the civilizing influence of the institutions in question; so that, upon the suppositions which I have made, the only issue to be considered is as to whether these benefits would be more than counterbalanced by the evils of offending the sense of Sabbatarianism which is assumed so largely to predominate among the working-classes. And this introduces us to the second and only other argument which was adduced by Lord Beaconsfield. He said: "In all questions into which the religious sentiment enters, it is highly desirable that no change should be effected that is not called for by the expression of a very predominant sentiment on the part of the people." If this means that legislation ought not to interfere aggressively with the religious sentiments of the many, it is, no doubt, a proper utterance; but, if it means that the socially harmless and even beneficial recreation of the many is to be prohibited by the particular religious sentiments of the few—and this is what it does mean if the words are taken to mean what they say—then I think the utterance is most improper. The idea which underlies this utterance seems to be that the religious sentiment is of so much value to the state that it ought to be tenderly fostered in all its ramifications, even to the extent of preventing reforms conceded to be beneficial, lest they should prune the twigs of the structure thus tenderly fostered. Now, I do not wish to enter on the question as to how far the religious sentiment is of value to the state; for I think it is quite obvious in the present case that, let us place this value as high as we choose, the contemplated reform cannot be other than completely beneficial. The workingmen who prefer spending their Sundays at home would not be injured by their brothers visiting museums and art-galleries; while, in so far as the religious sentiment is concerned, it ought to be a matter of gratification to all who entertain it that those workingmen who do not prefer spending their Sundays at home would, by the opening of such institutions, have an inducement supplied to turn their backs upon the beer-shops, and to bring their families to see the things of interest in nature, or the things of beauty in art. It is not that the opening of the institutions in question would act as a counter-inducement to that which is held out by the churches. Workingmen who are in the habit of going to church will, in any case, continue going to church, even though some of them may also spend their Sunday afternoons in the museums and galleries. And, so far as recreation is concerned, I am inclined to think it is not desirable that there should be any antagonism offered to the inducement which is held out by the churches. For I am inclined to think that the class of emotions which public worship arouses in a religious mind are of a high recreative value; and so, as a mere matter of sanitary interest, I should be sorry to see the churches interfered with by other institutions of a less recreative kind. But, in the present instance, the antagonism should not be museums and galleries *versus* chapels and churches, but museums and galleries *versus* public-houses and all places of loitering idleness; and any "religious sentiment" that seeks to oppose the introduction of such an antagonism can only be pronounced immoral.

Two other arguments against the reform were adduced in the debate, neither of which posaesses the smallest validity. The Archbishop of Canterbury argued: "What were their lordships called upon to do to-night? It was before the eyes of the people of this kingdom, to pronounce a deliberate opinion that the policy with regard to the observance of the Sunday hitherto pursued in this country had been a mistake... If any change were made, there was great danger of the day of rest being lost," as it would be the thin edge of the wedge to the introduction of other changes of a more advanced kind. Now, this is an argument which may always be adduced against any proposed reform, however obvious the need. We must not make the change because by so doing we should condemn the policy of the past and lead the way to further changes in the future. But, if a change is seen in itself to be desirable, such hypertrophied conservatism as this ought not to be allowed to obstruct progress. Moreover, in the present instance I am persuaded that the fears for the future are groundless. There is no necessary, or even remote, connection between art-galleries and music-halls; and, so long as "the religious sentiments" in this country remain what they are, neither religion nor reason will be able to trace a similarity or a precedent that does not exist.

The other argument to which I have alluded is, that the opening of museums and galleries on Sundays would entail a certain amount of Sunday work on the part of porters, etc. To this argument it is sufficient to reply, in the first place, that, if desirable, voluntary labor of so light a kind would be forthcoming; and, next, in the words of the Earl of Derby, who "did not deny the extreme importance of maintaining the day of national rest; but they must recollect that, wherever recreation was allowed, some labor must be thrown on those who provided it.

They permitted excursion-trains, etc,... and on the whole there was a great preponderance of advantage over disadvantage." As in most museums and galleries the porters and other servants employed on Sundays would probably not amount to one half per cent, of the visitors who would profit by their labor, I think that the argument may in this, more than in any other case of Sunday work, be set aside as absurd.

I have been tempted to dwell thus at considerable length on the question of Sunday recreation, because it is one that is now prominently before the public, and therefore I hope that a few words in season may help to hasten a reform which sooner or later is inevitable. As regards the recreation of workingmen, I have only further to say that institutions on the model of workingmen's clubs deserve to be encouraged in every possible way. Wealthy and benevolent persons could not do better with their means than to found such clubs where most required, and to endow them with a small annuity which would serve as a nucleus to club subscriptions, a greater number of subscribers being insured by the smaller amount of the fees. The Volunteer movement also deserves every encouragement, as supplying exercise and recreation to all classes at a very moderate cost.

Turning next to the recreation of women, I shall begin, as in the case of men, with the upper classes. And here, for the ‾sake of emphasis, I shall confine my remarks to the one topic of muscular exercise. For ladies, more than any other section of the community, have fallen into the habit of neglecting exercise, and I am sure that I cannot draw too dreadful a picture of the consequences which here arise from the too general custom. These consequences are all the more to be feared because many of them are of so insidious a kind that the root of the evil may never be suspected. It is not my intention to frighten any of the fair sex by unfolding a tale of horrors; so I will only say, in general terms, that I am quite sure among ladies there is no one source of disease and early death more prevalent than is this habitual violation of the best known among the laws of health. Consider for a moment what the life of a lady in town usually is. She rises probably at nine or ten o'clock, without much appetite for breakfast. Till luncheon she remains indoors, reading a novel or magazine, writing letters, or attending to her household duties. After luncheon she takes a little "carriage-exercise"—observe the unconscious irony of the term—pays a few afternoon calls, and returns home to afternoon tea. Until it is time to be dressed for dinner, there is another period of total quiescence, and the tedious operations of the dressing-room which follow are certainly the reverse of recreation. Dinner in pleasant company no doubt affords recreation of a mental kind were such recreation required, which in this case it certainly is not. After dinner, during the season, she probably receives an evening party, goes to the opera, or indulges in some other kind of amusement which keeps her in hot rooms with vitiated air till the small hours of the morning. At last she retires to rest, complaining that her delicacy of constitution makes her a martyr to headaches, languid circulation, lassitude, and feelings of sickness. Now contrast such a wholly unnatural state of things with the daily life of a country girl to whom exercise is felt to be a *sine qua non* of existence, and do not wonder at the contrast between her state of blooming health and the feeble stamina of the lady whose position requires her to adopt the habits of town life. Ladies will no doubt tell me that these remarks are trite, and that they all knew before the desirability of taking exercise. I can only reply, if "ye knew these things happy are ye if you do them." And why not do them? Why not make the duty of taking daily exercise as important an article in your social creed as the duty of returning calls? If you say there is no time, the answer is preposterous. Senior wranglers could never have been senior wranglers had they not found time for their pull upon the Cam; and by not making time for exercise you are merely shortening the time of your life. Every day you can easily find time for a ride; or, if you are not able to ride, you may take every day a two hours' walk with some companion or object to make it a pleasurable walk. Such companions and objects are not difficult to obtain in the town; and in the country there are several kinds of outdoor amusements—such as rowing, riding, skating, lawn tennis, etc.—which are happily recognized by the stern laws of etiquette as suitable for ladies, and which in performance are singularly graceful as well as highly conducive to good spirits. Dancing is also in itself an admirable form of exercise, though its beneficial effects are usually much more than counteracted by the late hours and excessive exhaustion of the ballroom. This excessive exhaustion of the muscular, but more especially of the nervous energies, may, in this as in all other similar cases, be properly denoted by the term which is the correlative of recreation—viz., dissipation. For although it has become customary to restrict the application of this term only to extreme cases, and to apply it to less extreme cases merely as a joke, both in etymology and in physiology the term dissipation is alike appropriate to all degrees of wasteful expenditure of the vital energies.

In recommending bodily exercise thus strongly, I speak of course to young and to middle-aged ladies; but I am sure that even here there are very few who could walk their five or six miles a day without fatigue. This merely shows to what a state of enervation their habitual neglect of exercise has reduced them. Such enfeebled persons ought to begin at once to give their constitutions some chance of recovery; they ought regularly to take as much exercise as they can endure without distressing fatigue; and in a few months they would be surprised to find how greatly the length of their walks may be increased, and with what immense benefit they are attended.

Women in the lower classes of society may to a large extent share in the recreation of their male relatives; and I feel confident that the more those kinds of recreation are encouraged which invite participation by both sexes, the better. Great additional enjoyment is infused into a holiday if it can be spent in company with those most near and dear; the heart is then most open to the best influences of affection, and family ties are closest drawn in hours of happiness together. Such institutions as the Crystal and Alexandra Palaces, where a variety of amusements are provided at a cheap cost in country air and amid aesthetic surroundings, constitute the best type of institutions for the healthy and improving recreation of both sexes and all ages. Of parks and public pleasure-gardens I have already spoken, and the desirability of preserving commons and heaths in the near neighborhood of large towns is generally recognized. I will only add that no time ought to be lost in promoting the suggestion recently made to the First Commissioner of Public Works by the National Sunday League—viz., that in all such places of public resort harmless refreshments ought to be plentifully provided. As a type of more strictly town recreation, that which is afforded by the Polytechnic Institution deserves honorable mention, and the sustained popularity of the Moore and Burgess Minstrels' entertainment goes far to indicate that a much more healthy tone might be given to the entertainments which are generally provided by music-halls. Now that Cremorne Gardens, the Argyll Rooms, and similar places of public resort are being closed, there is certain to be a greater pressure of vice thrown upon the music halls, and the increased demand for low, quasi-immoral entertainments which will thus be set up is only too certain to be supplied. It is greatly to be deplored that, excepting the "gods" galleries in theatres, there are now scarcely any places where respectable women of the lower classes can witness a public entertainment that is not more or less of a degrading kind. Philanthropists would do well to start in London several People's Theatres, where amusing dramas, part-singing, and other forms of innocent entertainment, would be sufficiently attractive to render the theatres self-supporting. I have no doubt that, if this were done, there would be a very marked distinction between the character of the audiences attending such theatres and that of the audiences which now attend the music-halls.

Before quitting the class of workingwomen, I must put in a good word for penny readings, mothers' meetings, window-gardening, and last, though not least, I should like to recommend some general and definite system for the loaning of books at a nominal cost.

We come now to the large and important class—children. It seems a mere commonplace to say that children ought to he allowed to run about and romp and play as much as ever they like or can. Yet this commonplace is far from having a common place in the usages of modern society. Among the upper classes children are much too frequently restrained from taking their full amount of natural play, either by preposterous ideas of genteel decorum, or by the respect due to expensive clothing; while among the lower classes the playground is too often restricted by the limits of the gutter, and even in the parks we too often witness the melancholy spectacle of children still a long way from their teens acting the part of nurse to still younger members of the family. To remedy these evils in the case of the upper classes there is nothing to suggest, except that fathers and mothers should cease to regard their children's clothes as of more importance than their children's health, and learn to estimate at its due value the responsibility of fostering the most precious of their possessions—these living, feeling, loving little ones whose capacities of life-long happiness are being molded by their parents' wisdom, or destroyed by their parents' folly. In the case of the lower classes, the *crèche,* or public nursery, where abundance of romping play is permitted, deserves the most strenuous encouragement. Children of all classes will play as they ought to play if only Nature is allowed to have her course without let or hindrance from artificial restraints.

But, as the only object in rearing children is not that of making them healthy animals, some amount of artificial restraint is necessary when the time for systematic mental training arrives. Nevertheless, as bodily health is the most essential condition even to mental training, the most fundamental principle which ought to guide the latter is that of supplying it with the minimum of cost to the former. Yet in school-life this fundamental principle is almost universally disregarded. So long as the general health of a school is maintained at a level compatible with work, and not below the level that declares itself by conspicuous "breakdowns," so long nobody cares to reflect whether the system of school discipline is in all particulars the best for maintaining the general health at the highest possible level. I will not wait to consider the disgraceful food which, even in many of our better-class schools, is deemed sufficiently good for growing children to thrive upon; nor will I wait to inveigh against the system of competition which, when encouraged beyond moderate limits, acts as a baleful stimulus to the very pupils who least require to be stimulated. But, confining my remarks to the one particular of punishment, I should like to put it as a question of common sense, whether it would be possible to devise any mode of punishing school children at once more fatuous, more pernicious, or more opposed to every principle of science and morality, than are the modes which are now most generally in vogue. Consider for a moment the practice of giving "impositions." It is not supposed that copying out a stated number of lines is an economical way of gaining information, so that even the plea of imparting instruction cannot be advanced as a benefit to compensate the evil of the method. And this evil is a very serious one. The object of all our methods in education ought to be, as much as possible, to economize effort; the mental energies ought, as it were, to be nursed, so that by their exercise they should lay up the largest possible store of information. But the mental energy which is expended in writing out an imposition is wholly, or almost wholly, profitless; and the amount of energy so expended is considerable—especially in the case of long impositions. For the whole punishment of writing out an imposition consists in the *tediousness* of the process; and tediousness, by the painful class of emotions which it arouses, is the most wearisome or exhausting of the influences that consume the nervous energies. It may therefore be said that in whatever degree the writing of an imposition is a punishment, in that degree are the nervous energies dissipated in a wholly useless manner. Therefore, to say nothing of the actual time that is wasted in the writing of impositions, or of the slovenly style of handwriting which this mode of punishment induces, my great objection to the mode of punishment is that, by consuming the nervous energies in a wholly profitless manner, it stands in direct antagonism with all the principles that I am endeavoring to inculcate. And still more foolishly wrong does this method of punishment become when it is united, as it generally is, with another and still more objectionable method—I mean the custom of imprisoning children during playtime with the express purpose of denying them healthful recreation. To shut up a child already weary with work in an empty schoolroom under a depressing sense of disgrace, is something worse than cruel; to the child it is a wrongful injury that does not admit of being justified by any argument; and, in running counter to all the principles both of physiology and of education, it is a sin against society. In most cases the time during which a child is thus confined is the only time in the twenty-four hours that there is an opportunity afforded for any recreation at all; so that, when the weary time of solitude is over and school again meets, the unfortunate victim resumes work with energies doubly exhausted. Even if a child had the stamina of a man, it would be impossible that mental work resumed under such circumstances could be profitable— the faculty of memory being quickly affected by mental fatigue. But, as a matter of fact, owing to the great rapidity of physiological changes in a growing organism, a child has much more need of frequent exercise than has an adult; so that, whether we look at the matter from a sanitary or from an educational point of view, I think it is impossible too strongly to condemn the practice of confining school children during playtime.

Of course I shall be asked what modes of punishment I would suggest as substitutes for the two which I have thus so strongly condemned. This question, however, I am not careful to answer. Even if it is true that there is a difficulty in providing other and efficient modes of punishment, I should not feel the difficulty to justify the maintenance of modes that are so clearly injurious. But, merely for the sake of giving an answer, I may say that, in the case of girls, experience derived from many of the higher-class schools shows that discipline may be maintained, either without any punishment at all, or else by such kinds as are more nominal than real. The difficulty in the case of boys is no doubt greater, but not, I think, insurmountable. Many kinds of punishment may here be devised which go upon the principle, not of denying muscular exercise, but of enforcing it. Extra drills or other compulsory exercise during play-hours are modes of punishment greatly to be preferred to those involving sedentary confinement, although I do not pretend to insinuate that compulsory exercise in the way of punishment has the same recreative value as voluntary exercise in the way of play. For my own part, I have no hesitation in recommending corporal punishment as on all grounds greatly preferable to the protracted, tedious, heart-sickening, and health-breaking systems which, in the name of humanity, are coming more and more into general use. But, however great the difficulty of devising or substituting other modes of punishment may be, I feel sure there can be no reasonable doubt that the modes which are at present so largely in fashion ought to be universally abolished.

The above remarks of course apply almost exclusively to boys' schools; and, looking to boys' schools as a whole, but little more remains to be said of them in connection with recreation. The John Bull spirit of this country is in favor of allowing schoolboys to play the hardy and vigorous games which require all the muscles to be brought into active service. The case, however, is widely different in girls' schools; so, before concluding, I should like to add a few words with special reference to them.

School-life is the time when, most of all, healthful recreation is needed. It is then that the organism, being in a state of active growth, most requires the purifying and strengthening influences of muscular exercise to be in frequent operation; and the development which the organism, during the years of its growth, receives, is carried through its life as an unalterable possession. Yet in the majority of girls' schools how miserable is the provision that is made for securing this development! Even in our higher-class schools the whole mechanism of their discipline seems to be devised with the view of stemming the healthful flow of natural joyousness by the barriers of tedious monotony. On all sides a schoolgirl is shut up in a very prison-house of decorum; every healthful amusement is denied her as "unladylike"; she is imperatively taught to curb her youthful spirits in so far as these may sometimes be able to struggle above the weight of a mistaken discipline; she is nurtured during her growth on the unhealthy soil of *ennui* in a depressing atmosphere of dullness; and, as too frequent a consequence, she leaves school with a sickly and enervated constitution, capable perhaps of high vivacity for a short time, but speedily collapsing under the strain of a few hours of bodily or mental activity. Now all this is the precise reverse of what school life ought to be. The only aim of most of the higher girls' schools seems to be that of turning out pupils with a superficial knowledge of a variety of subjects, with such accomplishments as they may be able, by hard practice, to acquire, and with a well-drilled sense of the part that a young lady is to play in the complicated tragedy of etiquette. Now it is no doubt sufficiently desirable that girls, and especially young ladies, should be well educated; but, in my opinion, it is of far greater importance that schoolgirls should leave school with the maximum of bodily vigor that a wise and judicious nurture can impart, than that they should do so with minds educated to any level that you please to name within the limits of natural possibility. I should therefore like to see all girls' schools professedly regarded as places of recreation no less than as places of education—as places of bodily, no less than as places of mental culture. And, if this is considered too strong a statement of the case, it must at least be allowed that far more permanently beneficial work would be done by girls, both at school and after they leave it, if more permanently beneficial play were allowed. At present in most schools, with all indoor romping sternly forbidden as unladylike, all outdoor games regarded as impossible recreations for girls of their age and social position, the unfortunate prisoners are restricted in their exercise to a properly prison-like routine—a daily walk in twos and twos, all bound by the stiff chains of conventionality, with nothing to relieve the dull monotony of the well-known way, and one's constant companion being determined, not by any entertaining suitability of temperament, but by an accidental suitability of height. Could there be devised a more ludicrous caricature of all that we mean by recreation?

Do we want to know the remedy? The remedy is as simple as the abuse is patent. Let every school whose situation permits be provided with a good playground, and let every form of outdoor amusement be encouraged to the utmost. Schools situated in towns, and therefore unable to provide private playgrounds, might club together and rent a joint playground—care, of course, being taken that the social standing of all the schools which so club together should be about equal. Some such arrangement would soon be arrived at by town schools if parents generally would bestow more thought on the importance of their children's health, and turn a deaf ear to all the qualifications of a school, however good, which does not provide for the proper recreation of its pupils.

Of course I shall be met by the objection that, by encouraging active outdoor games among schoolgirls, we should rub off the bloom, so to speak, of refinement, and that, as a result, we should tend to impair the delicate growth of that which we all recognize as of paramount value in education—good breeding. I can only say I am fully persuaded, by the results I have seen, that such would not be the case. The feelings and the manners of a lady are imparted by inheritance and by the society in which she lives, and no amount of drilling by schoolmistresses will produce more than an artificial imitation of the natural reality. Therefore, once let a girls' school be a little society of little ladies, and we need never fear that active play, natural to their age and essential to their health, will make them less ladylike than does the stiff restraint of the present system. Rather would active play, during the years of bodily growth, by developing the coordinated use of all the muscles, tend to impart through after-life that grace of easy movement which we all admire, but the secret of which is truly revealed only to the children of nature.

So much, then, for bodily recreation in girls' schools. As regards their mental recreation, I should begin by recommending less mental work. In most of the higher-class girls' schools, as in boys' schools, a great deal more work is required than it is either judicious or desirable to require. The root of this evil is that a girl's education is usually made to terminate at the age of seventeen or eighteen, and, as a consequence, she is expected to gain during these early years of life a sufficient amount of book-learning to serve for the rest of her days. In many cases it is, no doubt, unavoidable that a girl's education should end when she leaves school; but I think that, in all cases, education ought to be less arduous than it is in many of our girls' schools. Even if education is to end with school-life, it is better that it should end with a little knowledge thoroughly acquired, than with a confused and half-forgotten medley of many subjects. Not that I advocate specialty and depth of knowledge for girls. On the contrary, I think that the aim here ought rather to be that of generality and width—languages, elementary mathematics, geography, history, art, science, and English literature being all taught, but taught superficially, or without much detail, and in as entertaining a manner as possible. The point, however, which I desire chiefly to insist upon is this, that schoolgirls ought not to be made or encouraged to work beyond their strength. In most girls' schools competition runs very high; and I am quite sure that in very many cases the aim of the schoolmistress ought to be to check its undue severity, rather than to stimulate that severity by competitive examinations. I have myself known many cases of girls sitting up late, rising early, and working all day to win their coveted prizes—a state of things which is a sufficiently crying evil even in boys' schools, but which is a still worse evil in girls—worse because the physique of a girl is usually less robust than that of a boy, and because the schoolgirl is doomed to a smaller amount of outdoor exercise.

Now, if less time were consumed in girls' schools by mental work, more time would be allowed for mental as well as for bodily recreation. And, if the time thus gained were judiciously expended, I believe that, even as a matter of mental culture, more would be gained than lost. Suppose, for instance, that some time in every day were set apart for mental occupation of a voluntary kind—a good library of general though selected literature being provided for the use of the pupils, and the cultivation of art being allowed to rank as "mental occupation." In this way the more intellectual of the pupils would be able to receive that culture which only general reading can impart, the more artistic would be able to improve themselves in their art by additional practice, and even the unstudiously disposed would find in a standard novel a kind of reading less distasteful than Euclid.

And here, while treating of mental recreation among girls, I may add that school-life is the time when provision ought to be made for mental recreation in after-life. Be it observed that mental recreation is impossible unless there is a natural and more or less cultured taste for some branch or branches of mental work. Indeed, the capacity for such recreation is clearly proportional to the degree of such culture—an idealess mind being incapacitated for obtaining any *variety* of ideas. Hence the great importance of width of cultured interest, and the consequent duty of the heads of schools to ascertain the mental predilections of their pupils individually, and, in each case where such a predilection is apparent, to bestow special attention on its culture. If this were more generally done, I am convinced that the gain to their pupils in after-life would be enormous. We are living in a world teeming with interest on every side, but to make this interest our own possession we require a trained intelligence. It ought, therefore, to be one of the first aims of education to supply special training to special aptitudes, whereby the mind may be brought *en rapport* with the things in which it is by nature fitted to take most interest, and so in them to find a never-ending source of mental recreation. If this method were more universally adopted in girls' schools, ladies as a rule would be supplied with more internal resources of mental activity and cease to be so dependent for the stimulation of such activity on the mere excitement which is supplied by the external resources of society. But as it is, whether in the concert-room, the picture-gallery, the library, or the country walk, it is of most ladies literally and lamentably true, that having eyes they see not, and having ears they hear not, neither understand. Most ladies have a natural taste for someone or other of the many lines of intellectual activity, and if this taste were developed in early life it would grow with the knowledge on which it feeds, till in mature life it would become an unfailing source of pleasurable recreation. Yet in most cases such a taste in early life is not so much as discovered. For instance, how seldom it is that we meet, even among musical ladies, with any knowledge of harmony! —and this simply because they have never ascertained whether the study of harmony might not be to them a study of absorbing interest. Or, again, how very rare a thing it is to meet a lady who has even a superficial acquaintance with any one of the sciences; and how vast is the paradise of intellectual enjoyment from which multitudes of intelligent ladies are thus excluded! And similarly with all the other lines of intellectual pursuit for which a certain small amount of rudimentary initiation is required in order to ascertain whether they are suited to individual taste. So that, as I have said, one of the most important aims of a girl's, and also of a boy's, education ought to be to ascertain and specially to cultivate the branch of knowledge in which most interest is taken. Let us not suppose that by following this advice there is any danger of imparting to young ladies that singularly objectionable and not very easily definable character which is most tersely and intelligently conveyed by the word "blue." No one can have a more intense dislike than I have of the cerulean tint; but, wherever I have seen it, I have always been persuaded that it is the previous character which has tinted the learning—not the learning which has tinted the character. Only let a lady be a lady, and nothing but envious ignorance can ever venture to breathe the objectionable word, while cultured refinement in the opposite sex will always discover in the culture of a lady that only which adds to her refinement.

I have now said all that I feel it desirable to say on the principles and the practice of recreation; and I will conclude by adding a few words on what I may call the ethics of recreation.

Health may be taken as implying capacity for work, as well as to a large, though to a less absolute degree, the capacity for happiness; and, as duty means our obligation to promote the general happiness, it follows that in no connection is the voice of duty more urgent than it is in the advancement of all that is conducive to health. By maintaining our own health at the highest point of its natural efficiency, we are doing all that in us lies to secure for ourselves the prime condition for work—that is, the prime condition for benefiting the community to whatever extent our powers may be capable. And, similarly, by promoting the health of others, we are, in proportion to our success, securing to the community a certain amount of additional capacity for work on the part of its constituent members, as well as increasing the individual capacity for happiness on the part of all the members whom our efforts may reach. Therefore, I take it that, if we regard this subject from an ethical point of view, it is clear that we have no duty to perform of a more grave and important kind than this— thoughtfully to study the conditions of health, earnestly to teach these conditions to others, and strenuously to make their observance a law to ourselves. Now, of these conditions one of the most important is suitable recreation. For this is the condition which extends to all classes of the community, and the observance of which is, as we have seen, an imperative necessity to every individual who desires to possess a sound working mind in a sound working body. Hence I do not hesitate to say that one of our most weighty duties in life is to ascertain the kinds and degrees of recreation which are most suitable to ourselves or to others, and then with all our hearts to utilize the one, while with all our powers we encourage the other. Be it remembered that by recreation I mean only that which with the least expenditure of time renders the exhausted energies most fitted to resume their work; and be it also remembered that recreation is necessary not only for maintaining our powers of work so far as these are dependent on our vitality, but also for maintaining our happiness so far as this is dependent on our health. Remembering these things, I entertain no fear of contradiction when I conclude that, whether we look to the community as a whole, or restrict our view to our own individual selves, we have no duty to discharge of a more high and serious kind than this—rationally to understand and properly to apply the principles of all that in the full but only legitimate sense of the word we call recreation. Again, therefore, I say, if we know these things, happy are we if we do them. And if we desire to do them—if as rational and moral creatures we desire to obey the most solemn injunction that ever fell from human lips, "Work while it is day"—we must remember that the daylight of our life may be clouded by our folly or shortened by our sin; that the work which we may hope to do we shall be enabled to do only by hearkening to that Wisdom who holdeth in her right hand length of days, in her left hand riches and honor; and that at last, when all to us is dark with the darkness of an unknown night, such Wisdom will not have cried to us in vain, if she has taught us how to sow most plenteously a harvest of good things that our children's children are to reap.

Health and Recreation[2]

That all work and no play makes Jack a dull boy is one of those common sayings which we seem bound to accept, whether we like it or not. It is a truthful saying and an untruthful, a wise saying and an unwise, according as one word in it is interpreted, and that word is, *play.* If play really means *play* in the strict sense of the term, as it is defined for us in the dictionaries, viz., "as any exercise or series of exercises intended for pleasure, amusement, or diversion, like blind-man's-buff"; or as "sport, gambols, jest, not in earnest"—then truly all work and no play makes Jack a dull boy, and Jill a dull girl.

But in these days there is a difficulty in accepting the saying as true, because the idea of play, especially when it is expressed by the term "recreation," is not always represented in the definition I have given above. We now

---

[2] By Benjamin W. Richardson (1828–1896).

often really transform play into work; and our minds are so constituted that what is one person's work is another person's play. What a backwoodsman would call his horse-like labor, a foremost statesman may call his light of pleasure. How shall we define it? What is play or recreation?

Men differ, I think, on the definition of work and play more than on almost any other subject: differ in practice as much as in theory in regard to it. I have had the acquaintance, and I may say the friendship, of a man who lives, it is said, for nothing but recreation, or pleasure, or play. Such a man will rise at ten in the morning, and after a leisurely, gossiping, paper-reading, luxurious breakfast will stroll to the stables to look after the horses, of each one of which he is very fond. He delights in horses. Thence he will away to the club, will gossip there, read the reviews or the latest new novels, and regale at luncheon. After luncheon he will play a rubber, winning or losing several shillings—it may be pounds. He may then take a ride, or drive, or walk in the park, and have a chat there; or canter over to Kew and look round the gardens, or attend a drum, or visit the Zoological or Botanical Gardens. After this he will return home, and, ably and artistically assisted, will dress for dinner. The dinner, in accordance with his life, will be elegant, sumptuous, entertaining, whether he take it at his own table or abroad. After dinner he may probably go to a ball and dance until two or three in the morning; or, if there be no ball on hand, he may have another rubber, or a round at billiards, or a turn at the play, the opera, or the concert-room, with a final friendly chat and smoke before retiring for rest.

To this gentleman—and I am penciling a true and honest gentleman, not a modern rake of any school of rakes—this mode of life is a persistent pleasure, and to many more it would, I doubt not, be a perpetual holiday. To me it would be something worse than death. The monotony of it would be a positive misery, and I am conscious that many would be found to share with me in the same dislike.

Some will say that is all true enough with respect to persons who have passed out of youth into manhood, but that when life is young the distinctive appreciations for different modes of recreative pleasures are not so well marked out. I doubt, for my own part, this belief. It seems to me that in childhood the tastes for recreative enjoyment are as varied as they are in later years, with this difference, that they are not so effectively expressed. The little mind is ever in fear of the greater, and is often forced to express a gladness or pleasure which it does not truly feel. When children, left to themselves, are independently observed, nothing can be move striking to the observer than the difference of taste that is expressed in respect to the games at which they shall play. More than half the noise and quarrel of the nursery is, in fact, made up of this difference of feeling as to the character of the game that shall be constituted a pastime. In the end, on the rule, I suppose, of the survival of the fittest, the strongest children have their way, and one or two little tyrants drag the rest into their own delights.

I should, on the grounds here stated, venture, then, to say that there is, in point of fact, no more actual difference between work and recreation than what exists as a mere matter of sentiment: that recreation is a question of sentiment altogether, both in the young and the old.

If we could get this fact into our minds in our educational schemes for the young, we should accomplish at once a positive revolution in the training of the young, which revolution would, I think, be attended by the happiest change and train of thought in those who, in the future, shall pass through the first stages of life to adolescence and maturity. The search for amusements, and for new amusements, among the well-to-do would not be needed, since the mind from the first would be naturally brought to find a new delight in each act new called labor. The word "labor," in short, might drop altogether; the praise of labor, which is so often extolled, would find its true meaning; and the blame of play, which is so often unduly criticised, would have its proper recognition.

It has always seemed to me that in that once high though brief development of human existence; in that period, if we can believe that the art of the period came from the life of it, when the human form took its most magnificent model for the artist still to copy; in that period when the perfection of bodily feature and build indicated, of itself, how splendid must have been the health of the living organizations that stood forth to be copied and recopied for ever— it has always seemed to me, I repeat, that in that wonderful period of Greek history, so effulgent and so short, the reason why such physical excellence was attained rested on the circumstance that among the favored cultivated few, for they were few, after all, there was from the beginning to the end of life no such thing as work and play. Everything was existence— nothing less and nothing more. Every office, every duty, every act must have been an existence for the moment, varied but never divisible into one of two conditions, practical pain or practical pleasure. Life was an enjoyment which nothing sullied except death, and which was purified even from death by the quick-consuming fire, that the life might begin again instantaneously and incorruptibly.

If by some grand transformation we could in our day approach to this conception which has been rendered to us by the history of art, and could act upon it, we should, in a generation or two, attain a degree of health which no sanitary provision, in the common meaning of that term, can ever supply. If we could turn our houses into models of sanitary perfection; if we could release our toiling millions from half their daily labor; if we could tell want to depart altogether; if we could give means of education to every living human being—we should not remove care, and therefore we should not secure health, unless with it all we could also remove the idea of the distinction of labor and pleasure, the morbid notion that some must work and some must play, that the world may make its round.

In this country, so differently placed to the country of the great and the ancient nation of which I have spoken, it is impossible, perhaps, ever to introduce a joyousness like to that which the favored old civilization enjoyed. Our climate is of itself a sufficient obstacle to such a realization. Where the physical conditions of life are so unequal, where we waste in structure of body, whether we will it or not, at certain fixed seasons, and gain, whether we will it or not, at other fixed seasons, it is impossible to attain such excellence by any diversion of mind or variation of pursuit. For universal gladness the sun must play his part, doing his spiriting gently, but never actually hiding the brightness of his face. From us, for long intervals, his face is hidden. Under these variations of the external light and scenery around us we have to cripple our minds through our bodies. Our clothing must be heavy during long stages of the year, and our food so comparatively heavy and gross that half the power, which might otherwise go off in vivacity or nerve or spirit, is expended in the physico-chemical labor that is demanded for keeping the body warm and moving and living.

To these drawbacks is added the unequal struggle for existence, the partitioning off of our people into great classes, the millions of whom are obliged to work from morning to night, compared with the thousands who are at liberty to make some change in their course of life; the millions of adults who may be said to be tied to some continuous, monotonous round of labor, until the whole body lends itself to the task with an automatic regularity which the mind follows in unhappy and fretful train, with little hope for any future whatever on earth that shall bring relief.

From whatever side we look upon this picture it seems at first sight to present an almost insoluble problem, when the conception of mixing recreation with work, so as to make all work recreative, is considered. Among the masses there is no true recreation whatever, no real variation from the daily unceasing and all but hopeless toil; nay, when we ascend from the industrial and purely muscular workers to the majority who live by work, we find little that is more hopeful. There is no true recreation among any class except one, and that a limited and happy few, who find in mental labor of a varied and congenial kind the diversity of work which constitutes the truly re-creative and re-created life.

We get, in fact, a little light on the nature of healthful recreation as we let our minds rest on this one and almost exceptional class of men of varied life and action of a mental kind. They come before us showing what recreation can effect through the mere act of varying the labor. The brain-worker who is divested of worry is at once the happiest and the healthiest of mankind—happiest, perchance, because healthiest; a man constantly re-created, and therefore of longest life.

Dr. Beard, of New York, who has recently computed the facts bearing on this particular point, gives us a reading upon it which is singularly appropriate to the topic now under consideration. He has reckoned up the life-value of five hundred men of greatest mental activity: poets, philosophers, men of science, inventors, politicians, musicians, actors, and orators; and he has found the average duration of their lives to be sixty-four years. He has compared this average with the average duration of the life of the masses, and he has found in all classes, the members of which have survived to twenty years of age, the duration to be fifty years. He, therefore, gives to the varied brain workers a value of life of fourteen years above the average. By a later calculation, relating to a hundred men belonging, we may say, to our own time, he has discovered a still greater value of life in those who practice mental labor, seventy years being the mean value of life in them. Thereupon he has inquired into the cause of these differences, so strange and so startling, and has detected, through this analysis, as I and others have, a combination of saving causes, the one cause most influencing being the recreative character of the work. His observation is so sound, so eloquent, and above all so practical, that I can feel no necessity for apology in giving it at length. He is comparing, in the passage to be quoted, what he calls the happy brain-worker with the mere muscle-worker, and this is the argument:

Brain-work is the highest of all antidotes to worry; and the brain-working classes are, therefore, less distressed about many things, less apprehensive of indefinite evil, and less disposed to magnify minute trials, than those who live by the labor of the hands. To the happy brain-worker life is a long vacation; while the muscle-worker often finds no joy in his daily toil, and very little in the intervals. Scientists, physicians, lawyers, clergymen, orators, statesmen, literati, and merchants, when successful, are happy in their work without reference to the reward; and continue to work in their special callings long after the necessity has ceased. Where is the hod-carrier who finds joy in going up and down a ladder; and, from the foundation of the globe until now, how many have been known to persist in ditch-digging, or sewer-laying, or in any mechanical or manual calling whatsoever, after the attainment of independence? Good fortune gives good health. Nearly all the money in the world is in the hands of brain-workers; to many, in moderate amounts, it is essential to life, and in large and comfortable amounts it favors long life. Longevity is the daughter of competency. Of the many elements that make up happiness, mental organization, physical health, fancy, friends, and money—the last is, for the average man, greater than any other, except the first. Loss of money costs more lives than the loss of friends, for it is easier to find a friend than a fortune.

The contrast put before us in these forcible remarks is most striking. It is the key to the position in trying to unlock the secret as to what true recreation should be. These brain-workers of whom Dr. Beard speaks are, indeed, the modern Greeks, not perhaps in perfection but in approximation. The Greeks might, possibly, have gone higher than they did in the way of developed physical beauty and of mental endowment, and these happy brain-workers of later ages might, perhaps, more nearly approach the happy Greeks, But both were on the lines toward the highest that may be attainable, and this, as a means of indicating the right line, is my reason for using the illustrations that have been offered.

That which I have so far urged consists, then, of two arguments: Firstly, that recreation to be healthful must, as its meaning conveys, literally, be a process of re-creating; that is, of reconstructing or rebuilding; a practice entirely distinct from what is called play, when by that is meant either cessation from every kind of creation, or enjoyment of abnormal pleasures which weary mind and body. Secondly, that they who are able to live and re-create in the manner suggested are, in positive fact, they who present the healthiest, the happiest, and the longest lives.

From these premises I further draw the conclusion that we have no open course of a reasonable kind before us except to strive to beget a healthful recreation in the direction indicated.

At the same time I do not say this in order to divert attention from what may be rightly called the natural animal instincts of man. I have no doubt there might be a cultivation of mind which should cease to be recreative, and which thereby should be as injurious to the health of the body as an over-cultivation of mere gross mechanical labor, and which might even be more dangerous. It is not a little interesting to observe that the greatest of the Greeks had become conscious of this very danger, as if he had learned its existence from observations in his daily life. Plato, in treating of this subject in one of his admirable discourses, warns us against the delusion that the cultivation of nothing but what is intellectually the best is, of necessity, always the best. It is more just, he says, to take account of good things than of evil. Everything good is beautiful; yet the beautiful is not without measure. An animal destined to be beautiful must possess symmetry. Of symmetries we understand those which are small, but are ignorant of the greatest. And, indeed, no symmetry is of more importance with respect to health and disease, virtue and vice, than that of the soul toward the body. When a weaker and inferior form is the vehicle of a strong and in every way mighty soul, or the contrary; and when these, soul and body, enter into compact union, then the animal is not wholly beautiful, for it is without symmetry., Just as a body which has immoderately long legs, or any other superfluity of parts that hinder its symmetry, becomes base, in the participation of labor suffers many afflictions, and, though suffering an aggregation of accidents, becomes the cause to itself of many ills, so the compound essence—of body and soul—which we call the animal, when the soul is stronger than the body and prevails over it—then the soul, agitating the whole body, charges it with diseases, and by ardent pursuit causes it to waste away. On the contrary, when a body that is large or superior to the soul is joined with a small and weak intellect, the motions of the more powerful, prevailing and enlarging what is their own, but making the reflective part of the soul deaf, indocile, and oblivious, it induces the greatest of all diseases, ignorance. As a practical corollary to these remarks, Plato adds that there is one safety for both the conditions he has specified: neither to move the soul without the body, nor the body without the soul. The mathematician, therefore, or anyone else who ardently devotes himself to any intellectual pursuit, should at the same time engage the body in gymnastic exercises; while the man who is careful in forming the body should at the same time unite the motions of the soul, in the exercise of music and philosophy, if he intends to be one who may justly be called beautiful and at the same time "right good."

Such is the Platonic reading of the recreative life as it appeared to him in his day and among his marvelous people. We have but to trouble ourselves with half the problem he refers to, and with but half the advice that he suggests. Little fear, I think, is there among us that the soul should be so much stronger than the body, and so greatly prevail over it that it should agitate the whole inwardly, and by ardent application to learned pursuits cause the body to waste away. Nor is this to be regretted, because if the danger so stated were a prevailing one we should have two evils to cure in lieu of one which is all-sufficient for the reforming work of many of the coming generations of men.

I have not, I trust, dwelt too long on what I may call the practical definition of recreation as it ought, I think, to be understood, as it once was understood and practiced, and as it is still practiced, if not systematically understood, by a few whose varied and delightful works and tastes make them the healthiest and longest-lived among us.

It is well always to have a standard before us, though it be seemingly unapproachable, and the illustrations I have endeavored to supply of all work and all play, and of long-continued recreation thereupon, form the standard I now wish to set up for observation.

To make all England, and all the world, for the matter of that, a recreation ground; to make all life a grand recreation; to make all life thereby healthier, happier, and longer—this is the question before us.

Confining our observations to our own people and time, it may now be worth a few moments of analytical inquiry as to how far we, in different classes of our English community, are away from so desirable a consummation— the consummation of all human effort toward the perfected human life: the dream of some poets that such a life has been and will return— "Redeunt Saturnia regna"—the dream of many poets that it is to be, if it has not been.

The Registrar-General, with much judgment, due to long and wide experience of the component parts of the nation comprised under the title of England and Wales, has divided the community into six great classes, which classes are, in many respects, so distinct that they may almost be considered as great nations of themselves, having their own individual pursuits, habits, tastes, and, if the word be allowable, recreations. He describes for us — 1). A professional class, made up of governing, defending, and learned persons, and numbering some 684,102 persons, chiefly of the male sex; 2). A domestic class, wives and women of the household, and hotel and lodging-house keepers—a large class, the great majority women, numbering as many as 5,905,171— nearly, in fact, six millions; 3). A commercial class of buyers, sellers, lenders, and transporters of goods and produce, chiefly men, and numbering 815,424; 4). An agricultural class, cultivators, growers, and animal-keepers, the majority men, numbering 1,657,138; 5). An industrial class, mechanics, fabric manufacturers, food and drink producers, and purveyors of animal, vegetable, and mineral produce—a very large class, having in it members of both sexes, and numbering

5,137,725; 6). An indefinite, non-productive class; persons of rank and property; and scholars and children; nearly an equality of representation of numbers of both sexes; the whole class including a total of 8,512,706, of whom 7,541,508 are scholars and children—the living capital of the next generation of men and of women.

As we glance at these classes we quickly detect that what may be called their vocations are extremely different; that each class—with the exception, perhaps, of two, the professional and the commercial, with that part of the indefinite class which is composed of persons of rank and property, and which approach each other—are as widely separated in tastes and habits and inclinations as they are in labors and works. Looking at the education of body and mind in these classes as a whole, there is certainly little enough of symmetry.

Among the representatives of these classes which are best able to command the advantages of true recreation there is little sound attempt to use the privilege in a refined and reasonable way. The persons who have their time at command, and who belong to the most favored division, are divisible into two groups: a group which does no work at all that can bear the name of useful or applied labor, but which spends all its waking hours at what it considers to be recreative pursuits, which may be laborious, but must not be remunerative; and a group which labors industriously for the sake of return or reward, but which steals from time of labor regular intervals in which to follow out certain of the recreations which form the whole life of the first group, in strict imitation of that envied group, and in hopeless neglect of any recreation of its own better adapted to its real wants and best enjoyments. Each of these groups suffers from the course it follows. The representatives of the first kind lose much, since they are forever repeating the same to them pleasurable or automatic activity. The second lose, because, while they are ever repeating the same useful activity, they are only relieving that activity by repeating day after day the same automatic and imitative recreations. Thus both are subjected to what may be called the automatism of recreation. The automatism of recreation is bad in every sense, and it is specially bad in the present day, because of the quality of it, as well as the limited quantity. There is no such diversity of recreation as is wanted to keep the body in health by the exercise of the mind. With one man the recreation is all taken out in cards, with another in chess, with a third in billiards, with a fourth in debate or gossip on someone persistent topic of discourse or argument, and so on, for what may be called the in-door recreative life. Nor is it much different with out-door recreative amusement. Some one particular amusement claims the attention of particular men, and to this amusement the men adhere as if they had to live by it, and as if, in fact, there were no other recreative pursuits in the world.

This specialty of recreative pleasure or labor—for soon it becomes labor—leads to consequences which are often of the most serious character. The man who undertakes the recreation at first as an enjoyment, and indeed as a relaxation, is so absorbed in it that he strains every nerve to be eminent in it, a professor of the accomplishment, with a local repute for his excellence. The moment he enters on this resolve, however, he loses recreation. He sets himself to a new work, be it mental or physical; his mind becomes an emporium for the produce of that one particular culture, and he is in respect to that not far removed from a monomaniac. From the day that he is completely enamored of the special pursuit it is little indeed that he is good for out of it in hours apart from the common vocation of his life. He becomes fretful if for a day he be deprived of his peculiar gratification; irritable if he joins with others in it who are not so skillful as himself; envious if he meets with a rival who is better at it than himself; and often actually sleepless in thinking and brooding over some event or events that have been connected with the previous play or venture.

If the time at my disposal admitted the introduction of detailed illustration of the facts here referred to, I could supply from experience instance upon instance. I have seen an amateur player so infatuated with the game, which he originally sat down to as a relaxation, that he became for months a victim of insomnia. He carried the whole chess-board, set out in various difficult problems, in his brain, if I may use such a simile, studied moves on going to sleep, dreamed of them, woke with the solution solved, was sick and feeble and irritable all next day, followed his usual occupation with languid ability and interest, resumed his play at night with excited but not recruited determination, got more and more sleepless, and at last failed to sleep altogether. I have known more than one similar illustration in whist-players and in great billiard-players, and have seen the results of these so-called recreations end in the most sad physical disaster, when the pursuit of them has been made a matter of living importance, and when the player has ever had in his mind that pitiful *if:* "If I had done this or that—if I had made that move on the board—if I had played that card—if I had made that stroke, how would the case have been?" It matters little what the answer to the question may be—whether it be that by such a move, card, or stroke, the game would have been lost or won; the perplexing doubt is there to annoy, and it keeps up an irritation which imperceptibly wears out the animal powers and does permanent injury to life. You see men while still they are actually young grow rapidly like old men under this supposed recreative strain. They grow prematurely careworn, prematurely gray, prematurely fixed in idea and obstinate in idea, angry at trifles, baffled by trifles, and, in a word, young senilities.

In this busy city, in the great places of business near to which we now are, there are hundreds—may I not extend the calculation and say thousands?—of men who, in pursuit of the recreative pleasures I have specified, or of others similar in their results, are wearing themselves out twice as fast—and more than twice—as they are by the legitimate labor to which they have to apply themselves that they may earn their daily bread. It is the fact; and the observant physician, as he listens to the suffering statements of these men, is obliged in his own mind to differentiate between the assigned and what is often the real cause of that train of evils to which it is his duty to lend an attentive ear.

Thus, among the most intelligent part of the community—among the part that can help itself—there is no systematized scale or class of recreations that can be relied upon to afford the change really demanded for health. Nor are matters much improved when we take up the kind of change that is sought after by the same classes in the matter of physical recreation. When the Volunteer movement first came under notice, and for some time after it first came into practice, it was the hope of all sanitary men—I believe without any exception—that the exercise, and drill, and training, and excitement which would be produced by the movement would prove most beneficial to the health of the male part of the people at a period of life when the training of the physical powers is most required and often most neglected. I remember being quite enthusiastic at that change and its promises, and I recalled the other day an often-quoted paper or essay which had sprung out of that enthusiasm, and which I dare say at the time it was written seemed common sense itself. I can but feel now that the hope was begotten of inexperience. The movement has been a success, I presume, in a national and political point of view, but a careful observation of it from its first until this time has failed to indicate to me, as a physician, that it has led to any decided improvement in the health generally of those who have been most concerned in carrying it out by becoming its representatives. Certain it is that nothing affirmative of good stands forth in its favor, and I wish I could stop with that one neutral statement. I cannot in order of truth and fairness so stop, for I have seen much injury from the process. To say nothing of the expense to which it subjects many struggling men, to the loss of time it inflicts on them, to the neglect it inflicts at the fireside and home, to the spirit of contest of mind and fever of mind which it engenders; to say nothing, I repeat, of these things—all of which, nevertheless, are detrimental, indirectly, to the health of the men themselves and of those who surround them in family union— there is a direct harm often inflicted by the service, call it recreation if you like, which is not to its credit. The man who has advanced just far enough in life to have completed his development of growth, and to have lost the elasticity of youth, the man who has rather too early in life become fat and, as he or his friends say, puffy, the man who has, from long confinement in the office or study, found himself dejected and dyspeptic, each one of these men has passed into the ranks of the Volunteers, in order to regain the elastic tread, to throw off the burden of fat, or to find relief from the dyspeptic despondency. For my part, I have never been able to discover a good practical result in any of these trials; but I have seen many bad practical results. I have seen the partly disabled men, in the conditions specified, striving to do their best to keep alive and be on a level with younger and athletic men, and I have been obliged to hear of the signal and natural failure of the effort. I have heard of the attempts to meet the failure by the tempting offer and too willing acceptance of what are called artificial stimulants to give temporary support, and I have been obliged to discover in persons so overtaxed and so over-stimulated a certain heavy excessive draw on the bank of life, an anticipation of income which, in the vital as surely as in the commercial world, is the road to a premature failure and closure of the whole concern.

There are many who will agree with me, I doubt not, on this point; there are many men, and there are more women—for wives and mothers are far more observant and wise than husbands and fathers on these points—who will be able to bring their experience to bear in confirmation of that which I have spoken; and these will agree that to put men of different ages and of different states of constitution and habits in the same position for recreation; to trot them all through the same paces; to make them all wear the same dress, walk or march the same speed, carry the same load, labor the same time, move the limbs at the same rate; that to construct one great living machine out of a number of such differently built machines is of necessity an unnatural and, in the end, a ruinous process. There are some, however, who, while admitting so much, will put in a plea for the younger members of the community. They will insist that the younger men, the men who are from nineteen or twenty up to twenty-nine or thirty, may with advantage go through the recreation of training after the Volunteer fashion. The case is much stronger on behalf of this argument, but even in the respect named there requires a great deal of discrimination. A race of strong men may be bred, and a weak race may, by gradual development, be raised into a strong; but a weak man, born weak, can, through himself, be led a very little way into strength; while during the process of training he can most easily be broken into utter feebleness, so that the last of the man may be worse than the first. Hence, in training the weak into strong through any form of recreation, mental or physical, but specially physical, there must be a singular discrimination. In this instance of Volunteering as a mode of progress in physical health for the young there are dangers that ought to be avoided with religious care. To advise a weakly youth of consumptive tendency and feeble build, or one having some special proclivity to rheumatic fever, heart-disease, or other well-defined hereditary malady, to compete with other men of the same age and of athletic nature, in the same recreative exercise, is to deceive the youth into danger. To force such a one into violent competitive exercise, and tax him to the same degree of vital withdrawal day after day, or week after week, is to subject him all but certainly to severe, if not fatal, bodily injury.

I have selected the recreative exercise of Volunteering as a case for illustration of an important lesson, and I have made the selection, not because the recreation is special as a sometimes harmful recreation, but because more persons are concerned in it just now than in aught else of the same kind of recreative pursuit.

There are many other so-called recreations which are even more injurious to the feeble adolescent and to the enfeebled matured individuals, who seek to find symmetry of health in extreme recreation. Football is one of these recreations fraught with danger. Rowing is another exercise of the same class. Polo, while the fever for it lasted, was found to be of similar cast. Excessive running and prolonged and violent walking—in imitation of those poor madmen whose vanity trains them to give up sleep and all the natural ordinances that they may walk so many thousand miles in so many thousand hours—these are alike injurious as physical recreations unless taken with the same discrimination as is required by those who enter into the Volunteer movement.

As we pass from the freer and wealthier classes of the community into the less prosperous we find no marked improvement whatever in any form of recreation. We begin, in fact, to lose sight of the recreation that ministers to either mind or body in a sensible and healthy degree, and to see that which should be recreative replaced almost entirely by continuous and monotonous labor. The idea of symmetry of function and development between mind and body disappears nearly altogether; so that, indeed, to mention such a thing would, in some of the classes concerned, be but to treat on a subject unknown, and therefore, as it would seem to them, absurdly unpractical. To tell a country yokel that his body is not symmetrical in build, and that his mind has no kind of symmetrical relation to his body, were cruel, from its apparent satire. Yet why should it be? Why should ignorance and labor so deform any one that the hope of a complete reformation, the hope of the constitution of a perfect body and in it a perfect mind, should seem absurd? It is not the labor that is at fault. The labor is wholesome, healthful, splendid; it is a labor compatible with the noblest, nay, the most refined of human acquirements. Why should it be incompatible with perfect physical conformation of mind and body? It is not, indeed, the labor that is at fault, but the ignorant system on which it is carried out.

There is much difference, in fact, between the three classes of the community called the domestic, the agricultural, and the industrial, in respect to the work, the recreation, and the resultant health pertaining to each class. The domestic class as a whole is, by comparison with the industrial, fairly favored. The members of it lead, it is true, a monotonous life, and see often but little of the beauties of external nature, but they find in the amusements they provide for those who are about them some intervals of change which are, as far as they go, of service. Moreover, except in that part of the class which is engaged in disposing of spirituous drinks, and which pays a heavy vital taxation from the recreation springing out of that vocation, its representatives are not exposed to harmful recreations to an extreme degree. The domestic class therefore presents, on the whole, a fairly healthy life. The majority of its members are women and mothers; and, in the gladness with which they tender their love and adoration to the young and innocent life that comes into their charge, they find perchance, after all, the purest pleasure, the most enhancing, the most ennobling recreation, that, even in the midst of many cares and sorrows and bereavements, falls to the lot of any section of the great community.

The agricultural class, less favored in recreative opportunities than the others which have passed before us, living a laborious and very poor life, ever at work for small returns, and finding little recreation beyond that which is of mere animal enjoyment, is still comparatively favored. To the agricultural worker the seasons supply, imperceptibly, some delight that is beneficial to the mind.

These as they change, Almighty Father! these
Are but the *varied* God.
Mysterious round! What skill, what force divine
Deep felt in these appear: a simple strain,

Yet so delightful, mixed with such kind art,
Such beauty and beneficence combined.
And all so forming one harmonious whole—
Shade unperceived, so soft'ning into shade
That as they still succeed they ravish still.

The labor of the out-door agricultural class, blessed by these changing scenes which the exquisite poet above quoted so exquisitely describes, is varied also in itself. Each season brings its new duty: the spring its meadow-laying and sheep-shearing; the summer its haymaking; the autumn its harvesting and harvest-home, and fruit-gathering; the winter its plowing and garnering, and cattle-tending; with sundry well-remembered holidays which are religiously kept. There may be through all this continuous wearing labor; there is; but, as it is not monotonous, it is to some extent recreative, and the facts of mortality tell that it is saving to life. The agricultural classes present a mortality below the average in the proportion of ninety-one to one hundred of the mass of the working community. Moreover, there is hope for the agricultural classes in the fact that it is comparatively an easy task to supply them with a perfect roundelay of beautiful recreations for their resting hours. It is only to remove from them the grand temptations to vice in the beer-shop and the spirit-store, and to substitute for these resorts a rational system of enjoyments, to win for the country swain the first place in that symmetry which Plato called "right good."

The utter blankness, the blankness that may be felt, in respect to recreation is realized most in the millions of the industrial class who live in the everlasting din of the same mechanical life; who see ever before them the same four walls, the same tools, the same tasks; who hear the same sounds, smell the same odors, touch the same things, feel the same impressions, again and again and again, until the existence is made up of them, never to be varied until death doth them part. It is to this class—repining, naturally envious, naturally restless, and at this moment of time unsettled, mournful, and disaffected, to an extent which few, I fear, of our rulers comprehend—it is to this class most of all that the balm of wholesome recreation is most necessary, and for whom the absence of it is most dangerous. In this class there is no such thing as health. It is a blessing not to be found. You could not, I solemnly believe, bring me one of them that I dare, as a conscientious physician, declare, after searching examination, to be physically healthy in any approach to a degree of standard excellence. As a rule the average of life among those who have passed twenty-five would not be above fifteen years.

In these classes we see the effect of what I may venture to call the denseness of work, leading to mortality in the most perfect and distinctive form—work without any true recreative relief; work without anything changing or becoming recreative in itself; work relieved at no regular intervals for introduction of new life.

The greatest of all the *social* problems of our day is involved in this study of the manners and modes of thought of several millions of adult English people, all confined in order that they may labor, with no satisfactory relief from labor, and with no land of promise before them. The greatest of all the *political* questions of our day is also involved in this same study. The physician knows that the wisest of mankind, the most intelligent of mankind, are only half their former selves when they are out of health. He knows that health which is bad, but not sufficiently bad to prostrate the physical powers to such an extent as to cause inactivity of the will, is the most perplexing of all states of mind and action with which he has to deal. He feels thereupon a fellow-sympathy with the political physician who is called upon to treat the industrial masses in mass; to provide for their minds' health, to calm their excitement, to plant confidence in their hearts, and, most arduous task of all, to find out the way for securing for them those two grand remedies in the

Pharmacopœia of the ordinary physician, rest and change of scene, in pure and open air.

"They find their own recreations, these working millions," I think I hear someone say. They *try* to find them, would be the truer statement. They try their best, but they have found few conducive to health, many that are fatal. They are to be pitied and pardoned for these errors of their finding. What if they do discover recreation of the worst kind in the bar and saloon of the spirit-seller? Have they not the example of the wealthier classes before them, teaching that the same indulgence, in another style, is recreation? May they not ask how many other obtainable pleasures are provided for them, and whether many, too many, of obtainable pleasures so called, and so bad, are not positively thrust upon them? They have labored all day in monotony: where shall they go for recreation, and what shall the recreation be? If they go far away they are removed from the sphere of their labors; if they look near to their own abodes, they find not one true and ennobling pastime, but fifty that are degrading, and, at the same time, filled with every possible temptation.

I apply this to our own people; but it is, I fear, equally applicable to other peoples. Dr. Beard, the American I have already quoted, writes his experience, gathered in his own country, as follows: "To live," he says, speaking of the same classes, "to live on the slippery path that lies between extreme poverty on the one side and the gulf of starvation on the other; to take continual thought of to-morrow, without any good result of such thought; to feel each anxious hour that the dreary treadmill by which we secure the means of sustenance for a hungry household may, without warning, be closed by any number of forces, over which one has no control; to double and triple all the horrors of want and pain by anticipation and rumination—such is the life of the muscle-working classes of modern civilized society;

and when we add to this the cankering annoyance that arises from the envying of the fortunate brain-worker, who lives at ease before his eyes, we marvel not that he dies young, but rather that he lives at all."

There remains still in the list of classes requiring recreation, and the health that springs from it, the last or indefinite class. Of the purely indefinite of these I need not speak; for they, the waifs and strays of our civilization, are, I fear, under little influence of such refining agencies as we would put forward for the future.